Disney characters and artwork © Disney Enterprises, Inc.

ISBN 978-1-4234-3937-0

Walt Disney Music Company
Wonderland Music Company, Inc.

DISTRIBUTED BY

HAL•LEONARD®
CORPORATION

7777 W. BLUEMOUND RD. P.O. BOX 13819 MILWAUKEE, WI 53213

Visit Hal Leonard Online at
www.halleonard.com

contents

Hannah Montana2

Meet Miley Cyrus

WE GOT THE PARTY

Words and Music by
KARA DioGUARDI

kick-in' it to-geth-er; it's so good to be free._____ We got each oth-er and

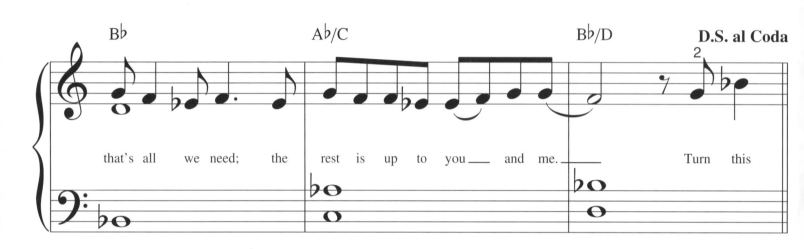

that's all we need; the rest is up to you___ and me._____ Turn this

CODA

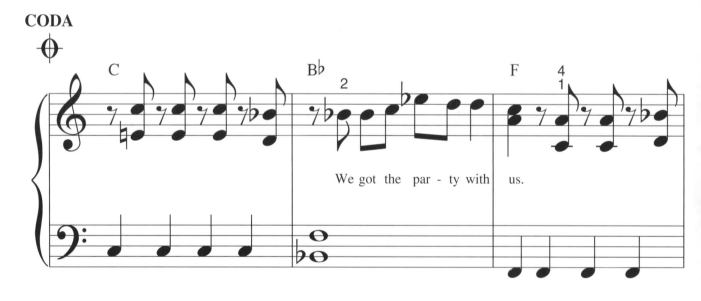

We got the par-ty with us.

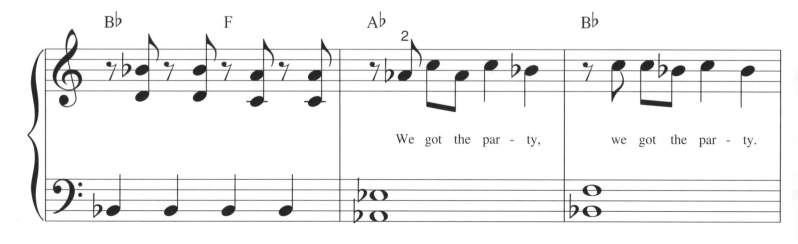

We got the par-ty, we got the par-ty.

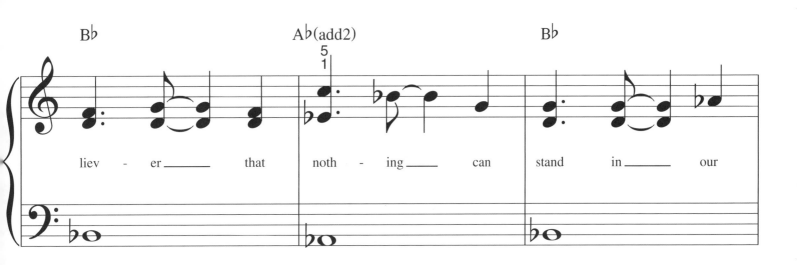

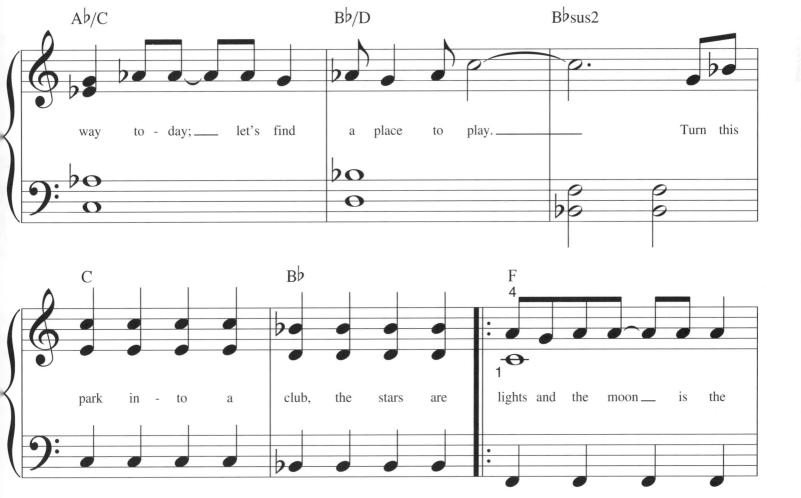

NOBODY'S PERFECT

Words and Music by MATTHEW GERRARD
and ROBBIE NEVIL

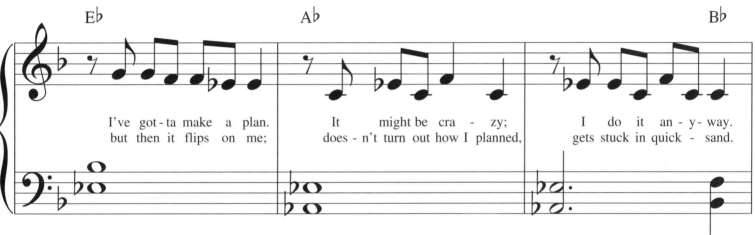

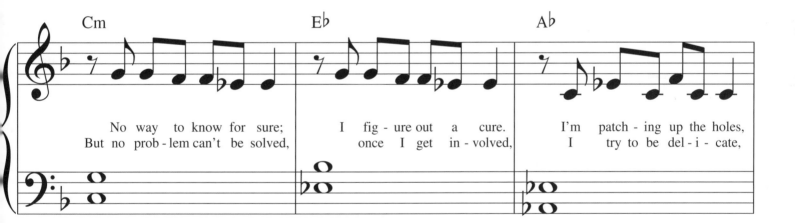

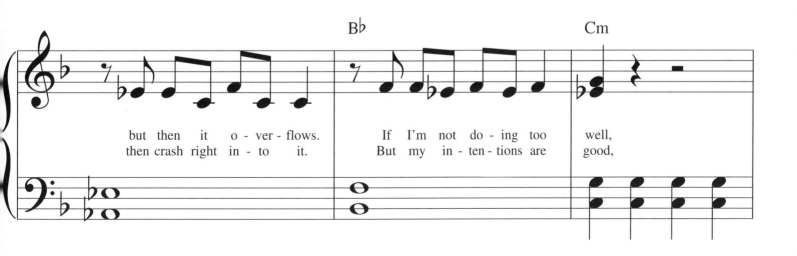

MAKE SOME NOISE

Words and Music by ANDY DODD
and ADAM WATTS

ROCK STAR

Words and Music by JEANNIE LURIE,
ARIS ARCHONTIS and CHEN NEEMAN

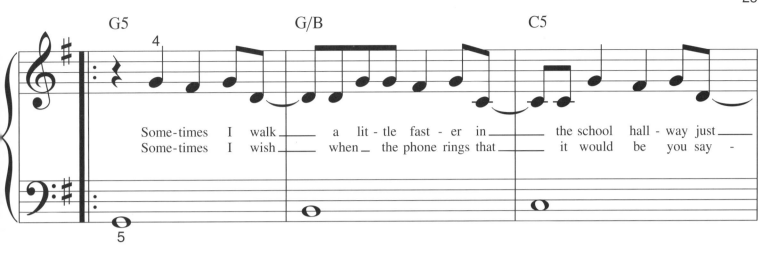

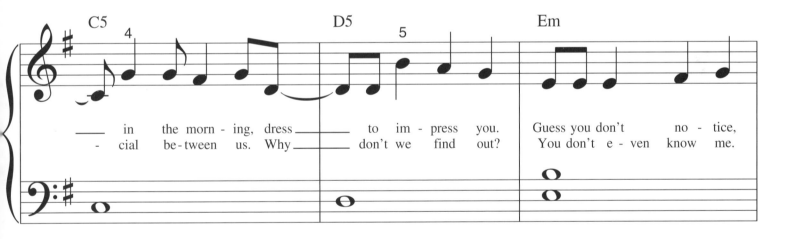

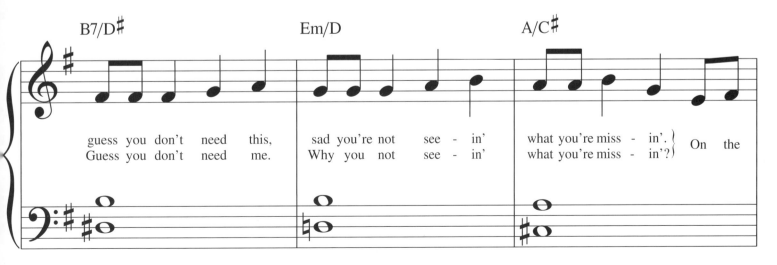

be, that would - n't it be nice if you ___ could see that I real - ly am a

rock star, yeah, ___ yeah?

Yeah, I real - ly am a

rock star. ___

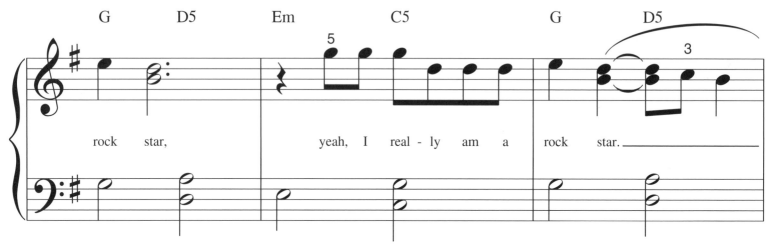

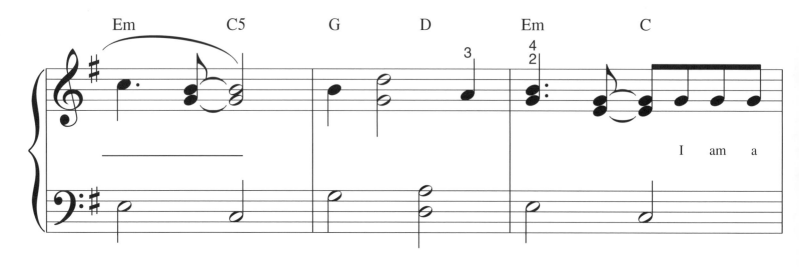

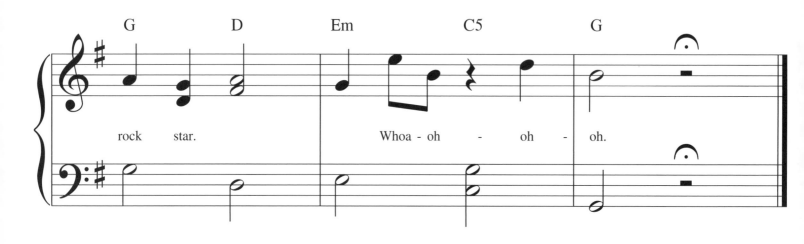

ONE IN A MILLION

Words and Music by TOBY GAD
and NEGIN DJAFARI

How did I get _____ here? I turned a-round _____ and there you were. I did-n't think twice or

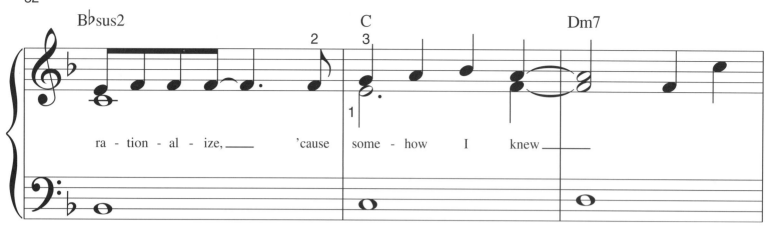

ra - tion - al - ize, ____ 'cause some - how I knew ____

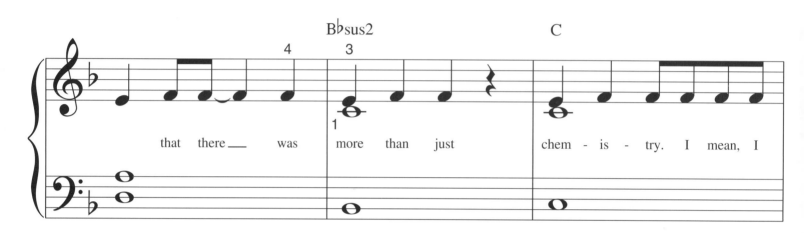

that there ____ was more than just chem - is - try. I mean, I

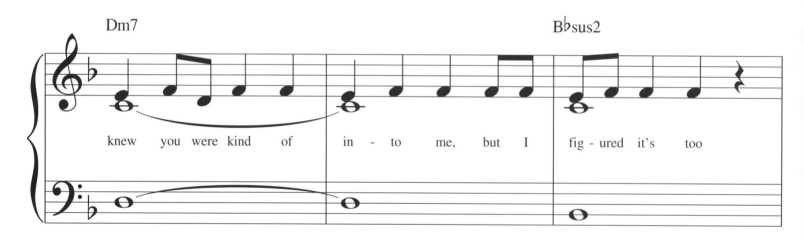

knew you were kind of in - to me, but I fig - ured it's too

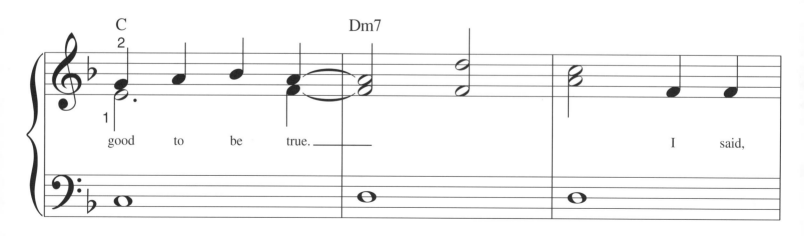

good to be true. ____ I said,

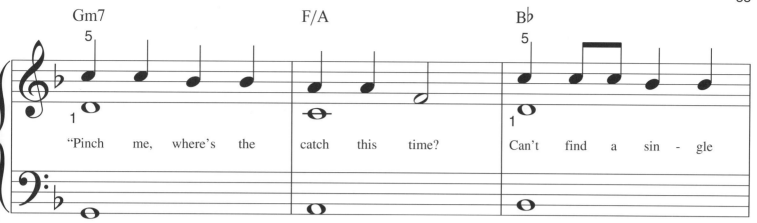

"Pinch me, where's the catch this time? catch this time? Can't find a sin - gle

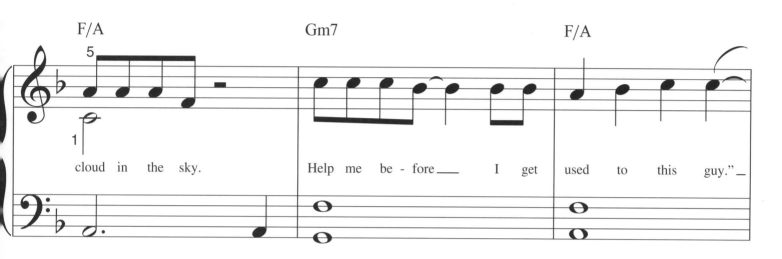

cloud in the sky. Help me be - fore___ I get used to this guy."___

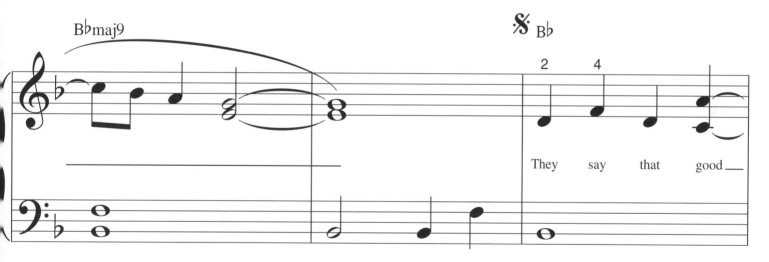

They say that good___

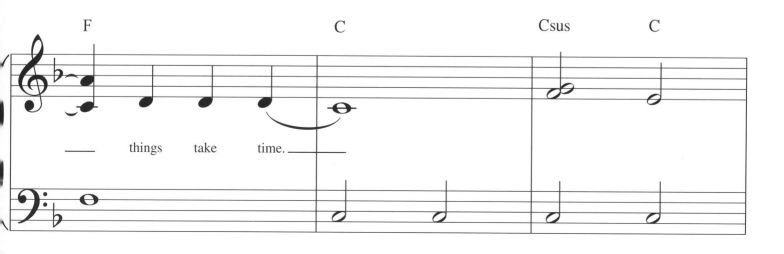

___ things take time.___

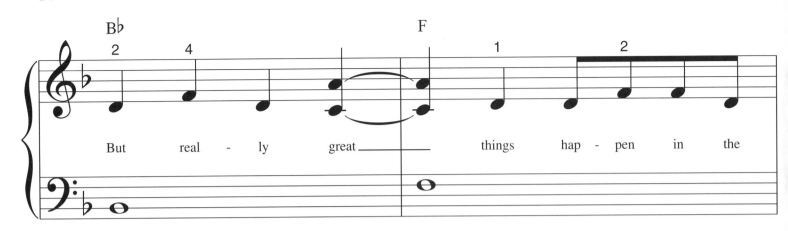

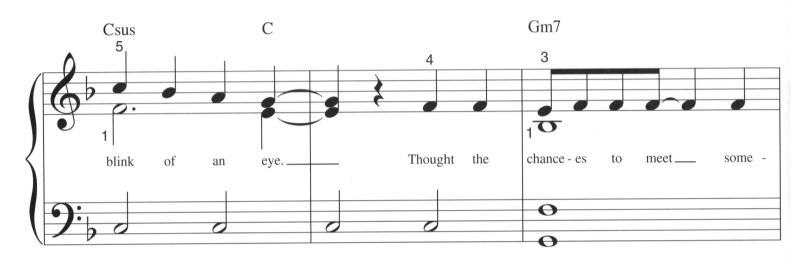

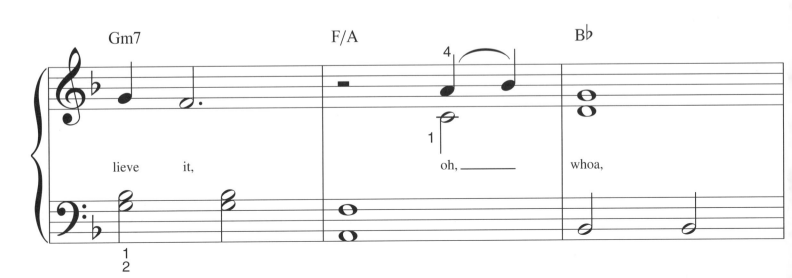

you're one in a mil - lion.

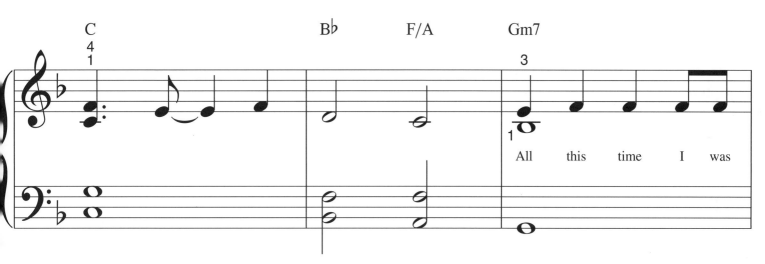

All this time I was

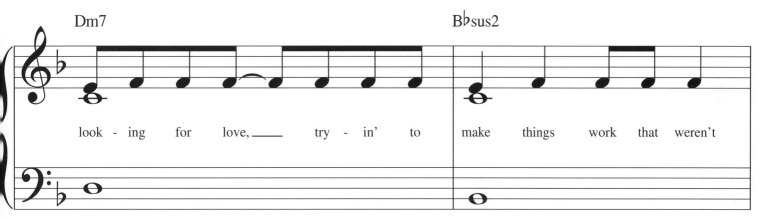

look - ing for love,____ try - in' to make things work that weren't

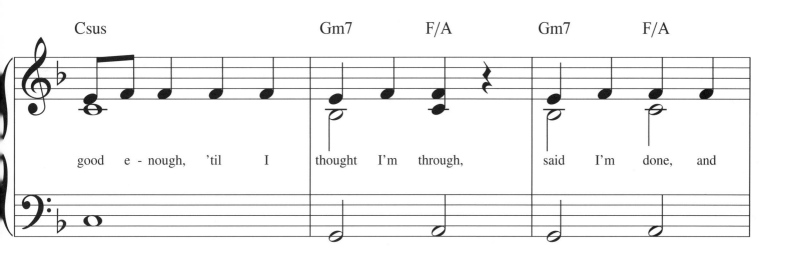

good e - nough, 'til I thought I'm through, said I'm done, and

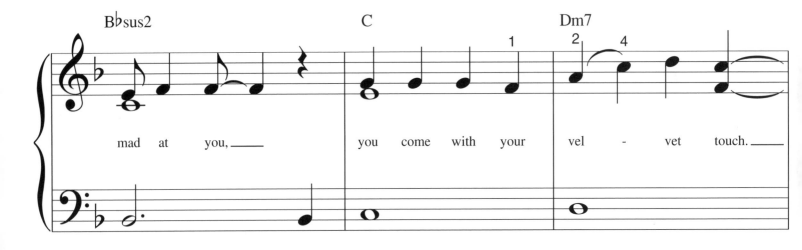

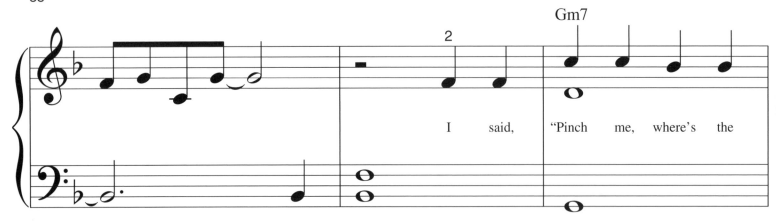

I said, "Pinch me, where's the

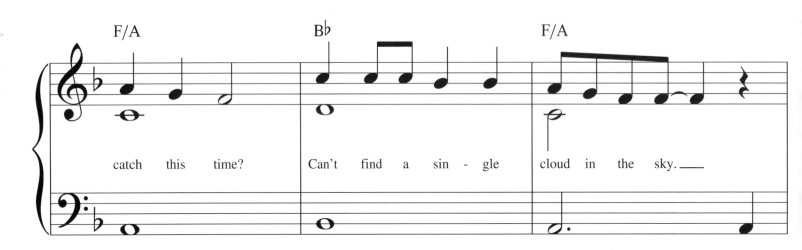

catch this time? Can't find a sin - gle cloud in the sky.___

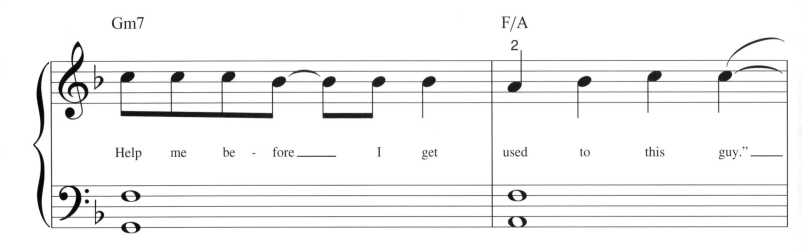

Help me be - fore___ I get used to this guy."___

They say that good___

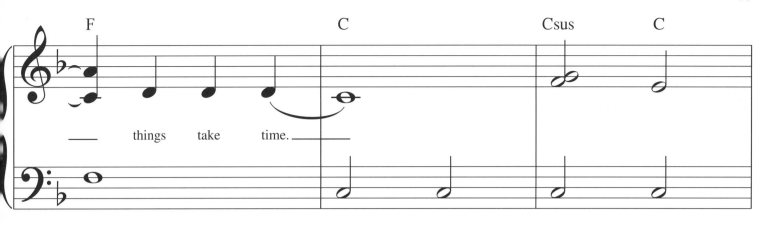

things take time.

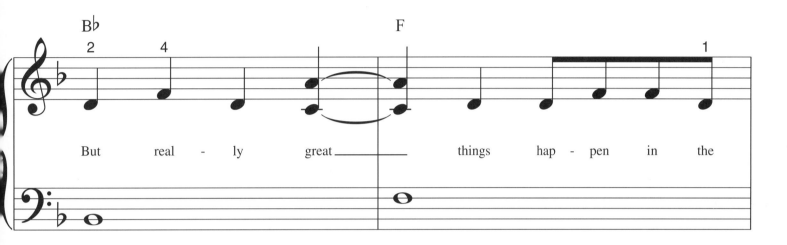

But real - ly great things hap - pen in the

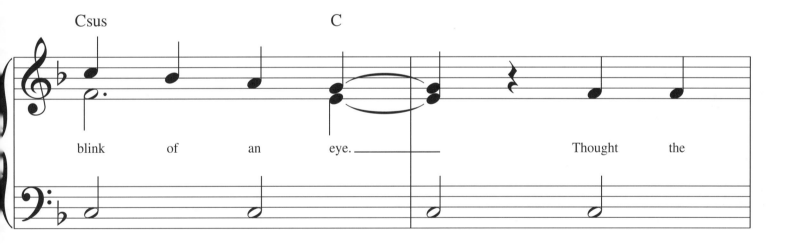

blink of an eye. Thought the

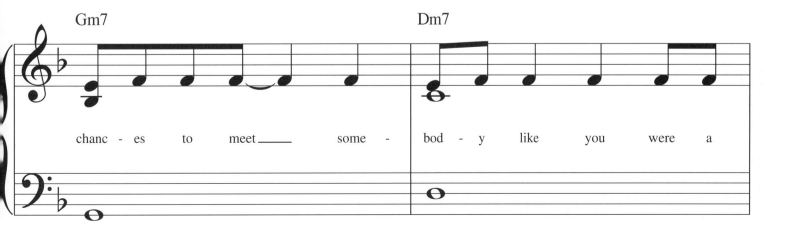

chanc - es to meet some - bod - y like you were a

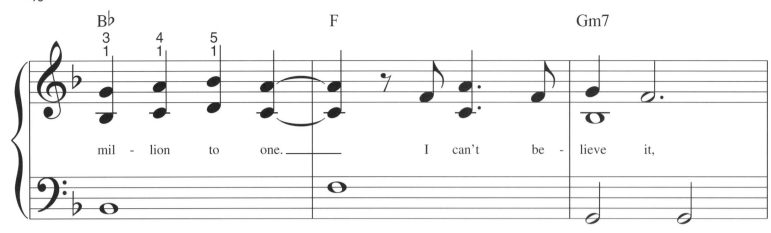

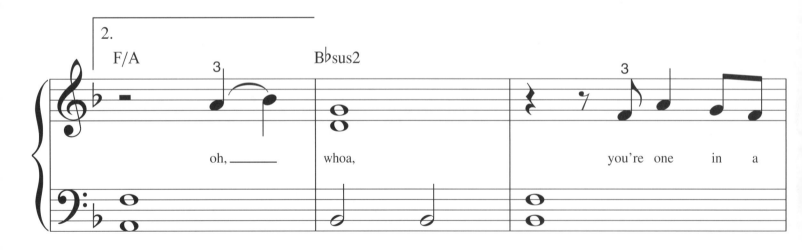

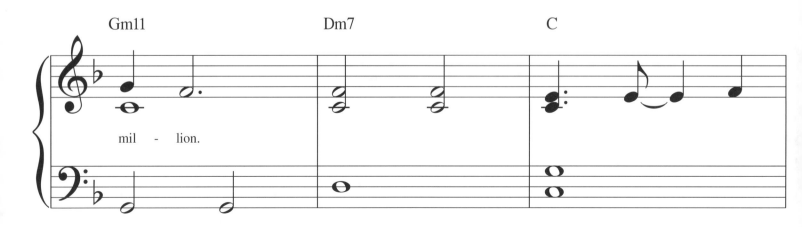

One in a mil - lion.

You're one in a mil - lion.

rit.

OLD BLUE JEANS

Words and Music by MICHAEL BRADFORD
and PAM SHEYNE

LIFE'S WHAT YOU MAKE IT

Words and Music by MATTHEW GERRARD
and ROBBIE NEVIL

50

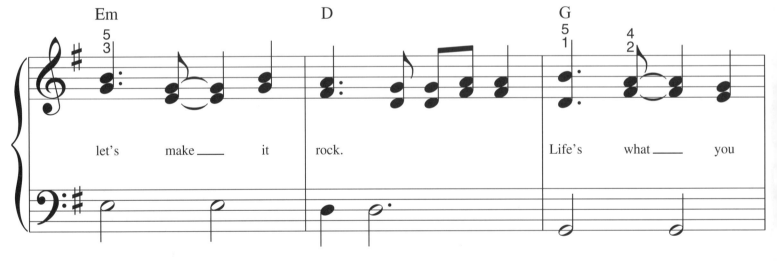

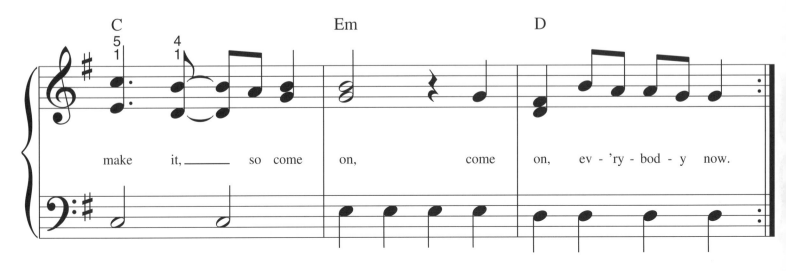

54

BIGGER THAN US

Words and Music by TIM JAMES
and ANTONINA ARMATO

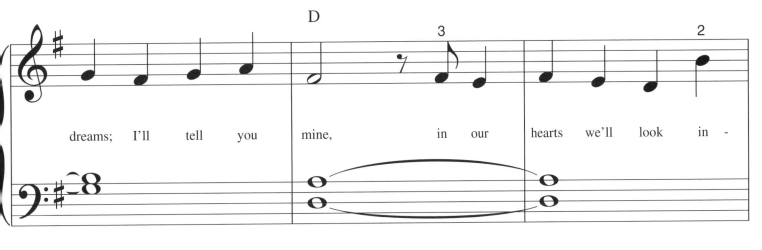

dreams; I'll tell you mine, in our hearts we'll look in -

side and see ____ all the col - ors of the rain - bow.

I know. We all want to be - lieve ____ in love.

We all want to be - lieve ____ in some - thing ____

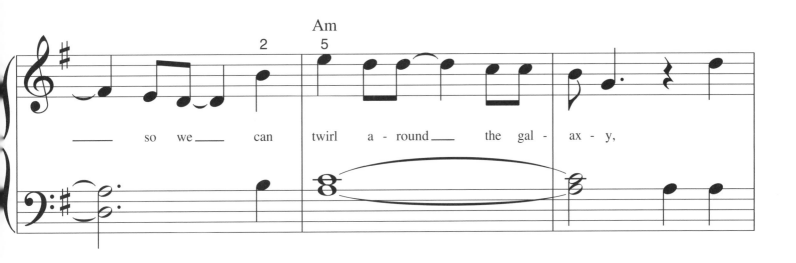

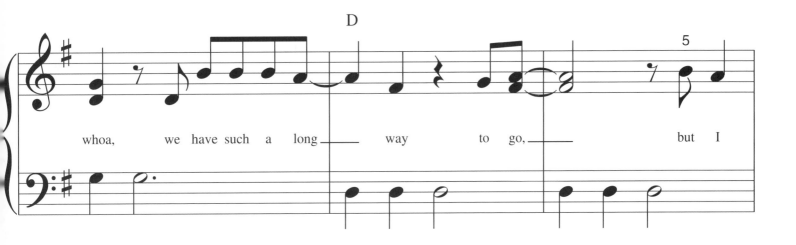

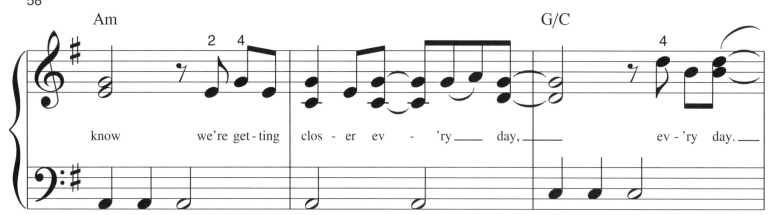

Am   G/C

know   we're get-ting   clos - er ev - 'ry ___ day, ___   ev - 'ry day. ___

D.S. al Coda

CODA

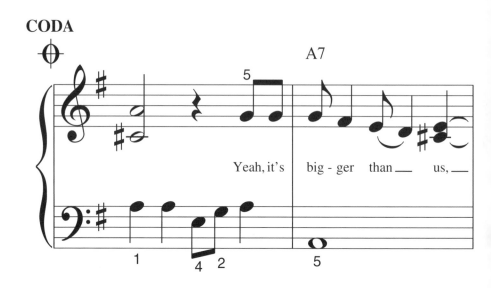

A7

Yeah, it's   big - ger than ___ us, ___

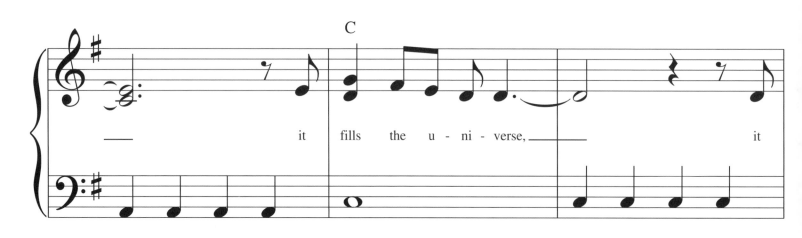

C

___   it   fills   the   u - ni - verse, ___   it

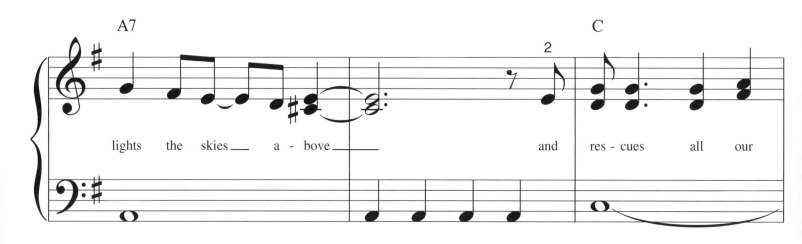

A7   C

lights the skies ___ a - bove ___   and   res - cues   all   our

YOU AND ME TOGETHER

Words and Music by
JAMIE HOUSTON

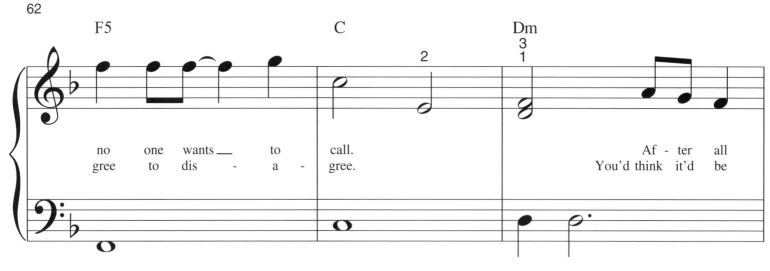

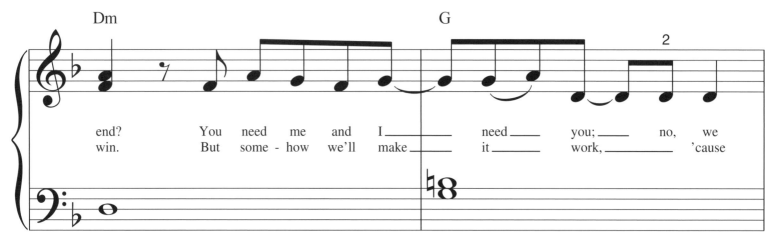

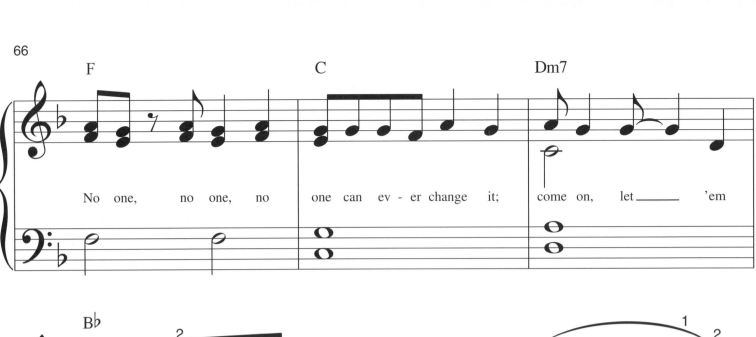

No one, no one, no one can ev - er change it; come on, let_____ 'em

try. Come on, let_____ 'em try._____

D.S. al Coda

It's you____

CODA

now,_____

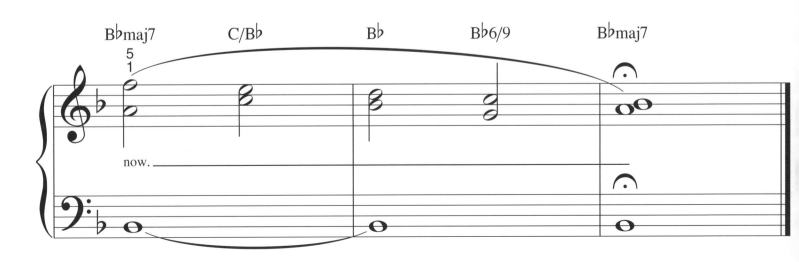

now._____

TRUE FRIEND

Words and Music by
JEANNIE LURIE

We sign our cards and let - ters, "B. F. F."

You've got a mil - lion ways to make me laugh.

You're look - in' out for me, you've got my back. It's so good

EAST NORTHUMBERLAND HIGH

Words and Music by SAMANTHA JO MOORE,
TIM JAMES and ANTONINA ARMATO

Uptempo Rock Shuffle

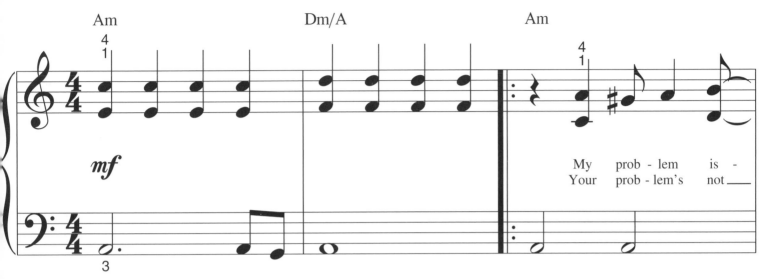

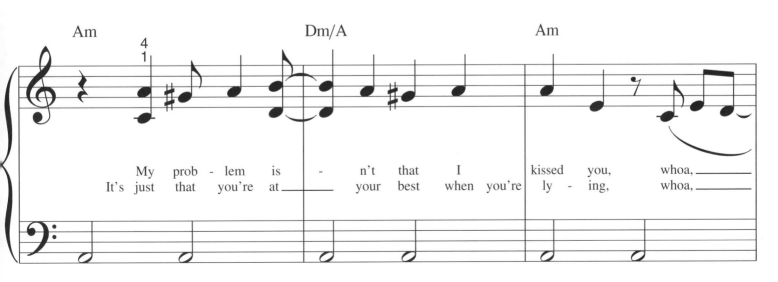

74

I guess, if I was stuck at East North - um - ber - land High for the rest of my life. ___

___ But peo - ple change: ___ thank God I did. ___

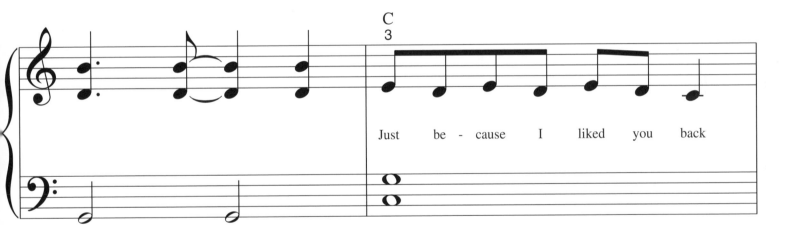

Just be - cause I liked you back

then, it does - n't mean I like ___ you now. ___

Just be-cause I liked you back then, it does-n't mean I like you.

can't go back; it's all ___ in the past. Guess ___ you got - ta laugh at it. ___

___

You're my type of guy, ___
if there's some con - fu -

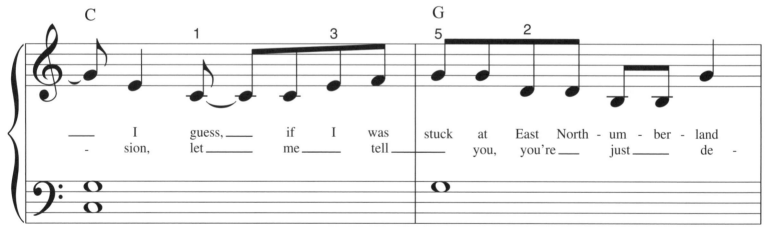

___ I guess, ___ if I was stuck at East North - um - ber - land
- sion, let ___ me ___ tell ___ you, you're ___ just ___ de -

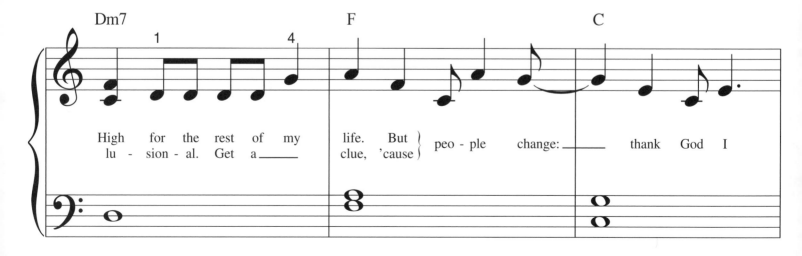

High for the rest of my life. But } peo - ple change: ___ thank God I
lu - sion - al. Get a ___ clue, 'cause }

LET'S DANCE

Words and Music by DESTINY HOPE CYRUS,
TIM JAMES and ANTONINA ARMATO

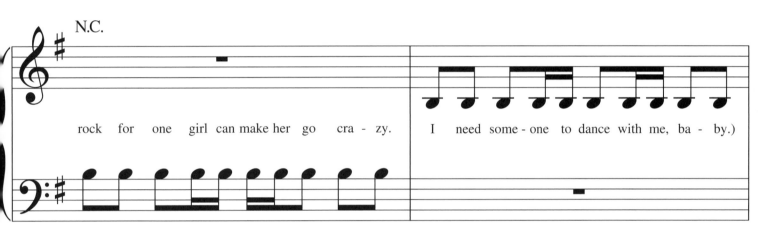

SEE YOU AGAIN

Words and Music by DESTINY HOPE CYRUS,
TIM JAMES and ANTONINA ARMATO

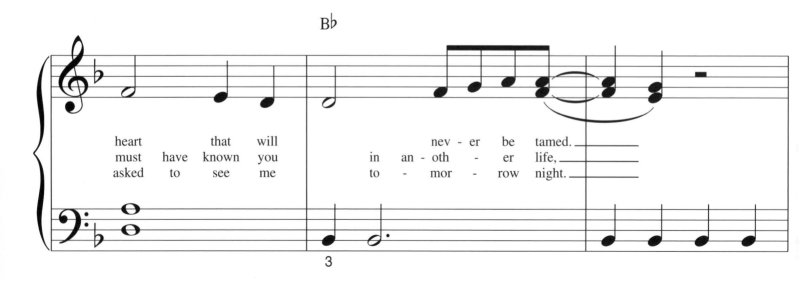

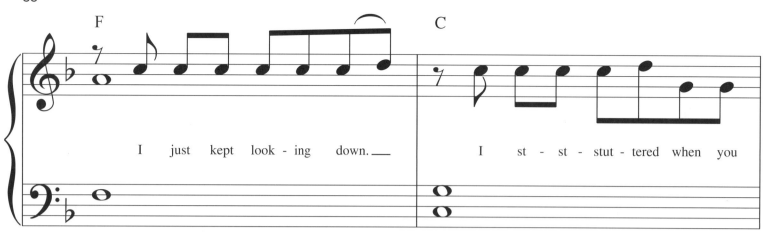

I just kept look-ing down. ___

I st - st - st - stut-tered when you

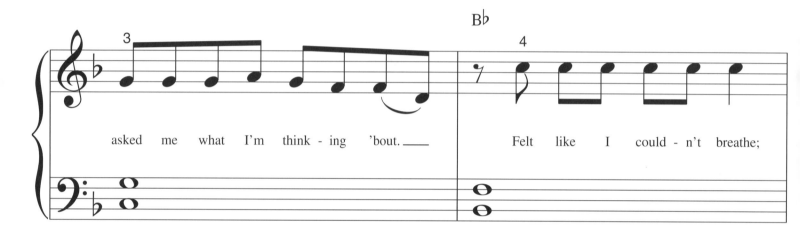

asked me what I'm think-ing 'bout. ___

Felt like I could-n't breathe;

you asked what's wrong with me. ___

My best friend, Les - ley, said, "Oh,

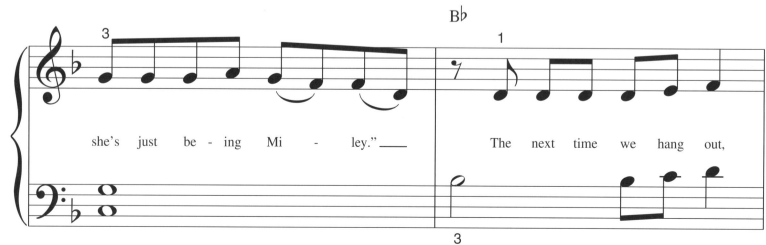

she's just be - ing Mi - ley." ___

The next time we hang out,

3

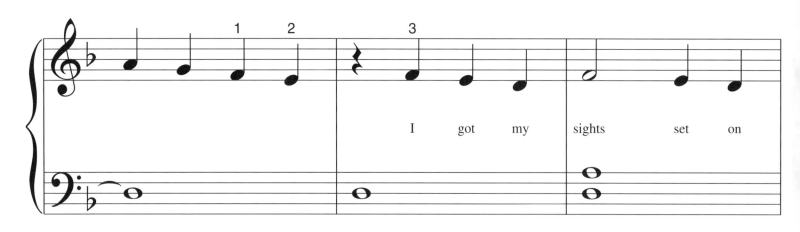

G.N.O.
(Girl's Night Out)

Words and Music by MATTHEW WILDER
and TAMARA DUNN

Don't call me, leave ___ me a - lone.
I'm out to have ___ a good time,

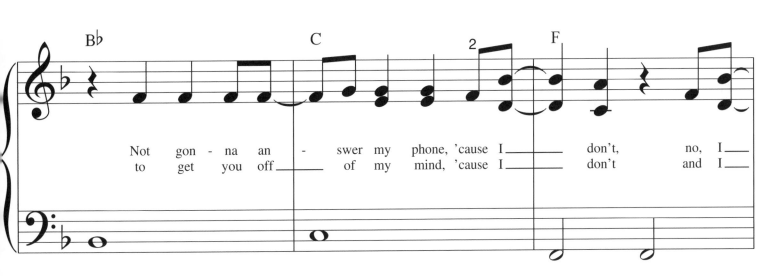

Not gon - na an - swer my phone, 'cause I ___ don't, no, I ___
to get you off ___ of my mind, 'cause I ___ don't and I ___

RIGHT HERE

Words and Music by DESTINY HOPE CYRUS,
TIM JAMES and ANTONINA ARMATO

AS I AM

Words and Music by DESTINY HOPE CYRUS,
ALEXANDER BARRY and SHELLY PEIKEN

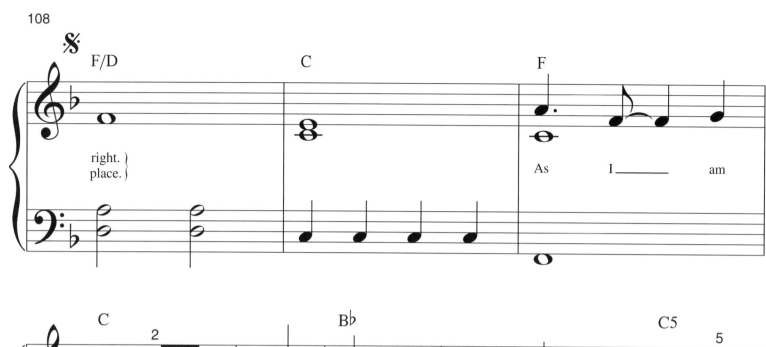

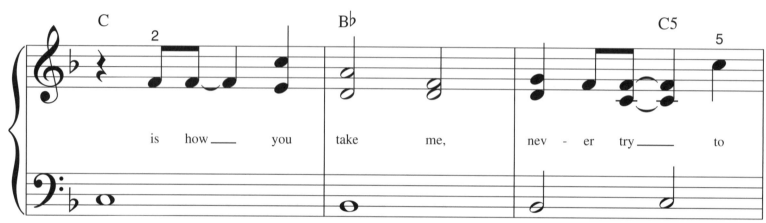

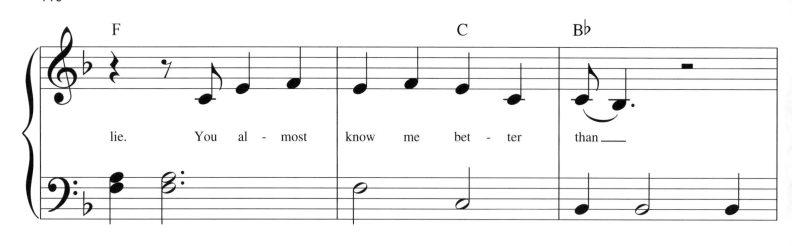

lie. You al - most know me bet - ter than ____

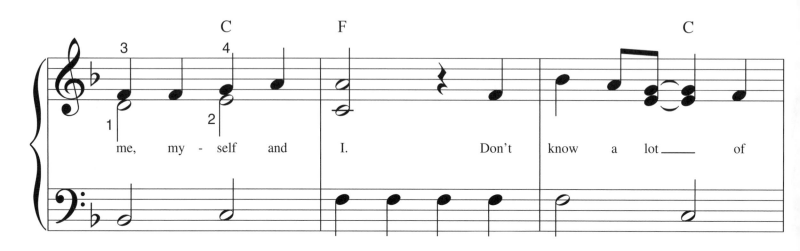

me, my - self and I. Don't know a lot ____ of

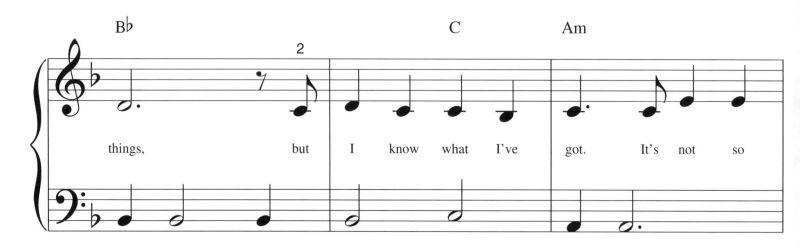

things, but I know what I've got. It's not so

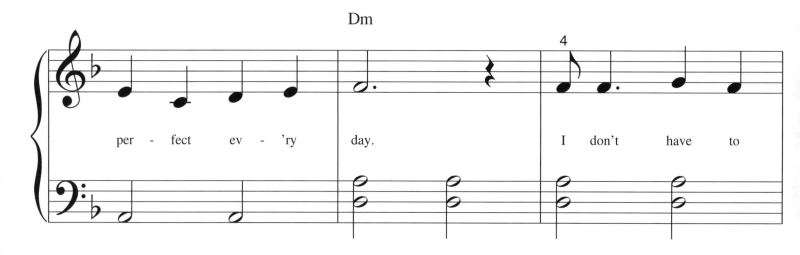

per - fect ev - 'ry day. I don't have to

care._____

You're stand - ing there,____

see - ing me for the first time._____

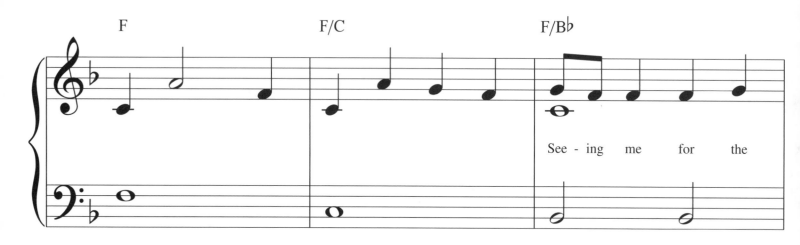

See - ing me for the

first _____ time,_____

see - ing me for the first time. As I _____ am

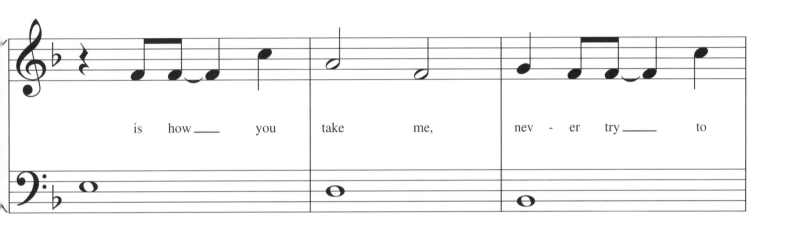

is how ___ you take me, nev - er try ___ to

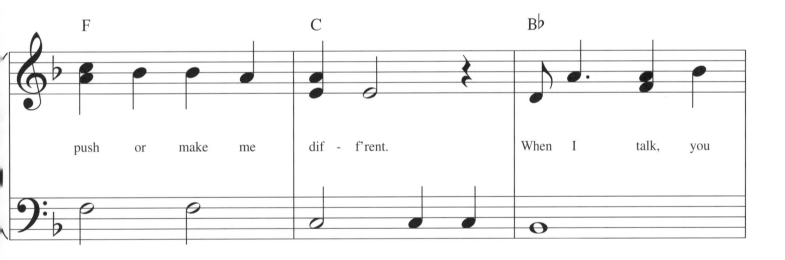

push or make me dif - f'rent. When I talk, you

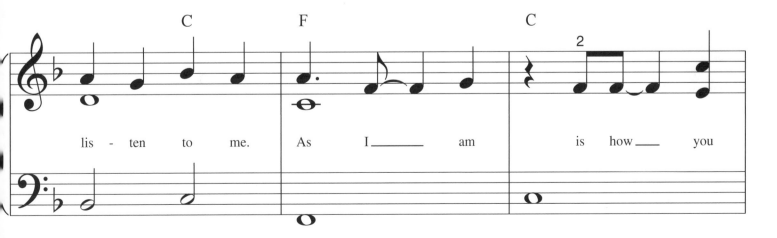

lis - ten to me. As I _____ am is how ___ you

START ALL OVER

Words and Music by FEFE DOBSON,
SCOTT CUTLER and ANNE PREVIN

CLEAR

Words and Music by DESTINY HOPE CYRUS,
ALEXANDER BARRY and SHELLY PEIKEN

six a. - m.,＿ and I'm | wide a - wake, 'cause I can't＿
did I smile＿ when I | hurt in - side? Said I was＿

It's

GOOD AND BROKEN

Words and Music by DESTINY HOPE CYRUS,
TIM JAMES and ANTONINA ARMATO

Moderately fast

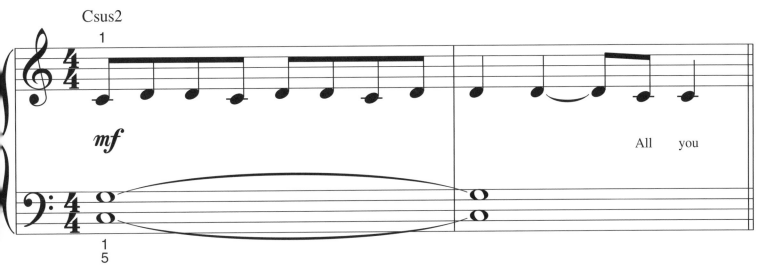

All you

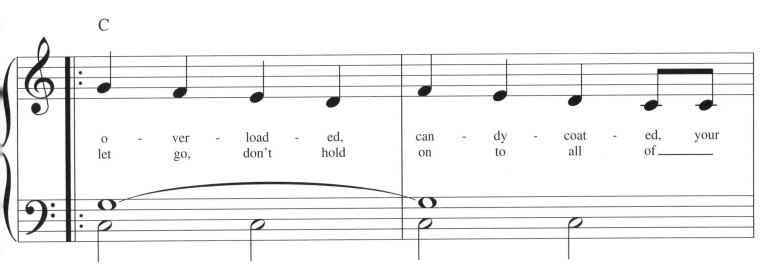

o - ver - load - ed, can - dy - coat - ed, your
let go, don't hold on to all of _____

life's im - plod - ing now. There's a risk worth tak - ing, a
life's _____ hard - est parts. When we think of stop - ping, let's

128

F

G

D.S. al Coda

to be - lieve in, just tell your - self,_____ "We can."

CODA

C

Dm

B♭

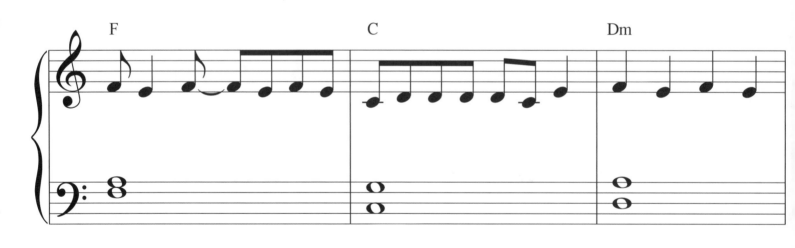

F

C

Dm

B♭

F

C

Get off your seat, on your feet,

I MISS YOU

Words and Music by DESTINY HOPE CYRUS,
BRIAN GREEN and WENDI FOY GREEN

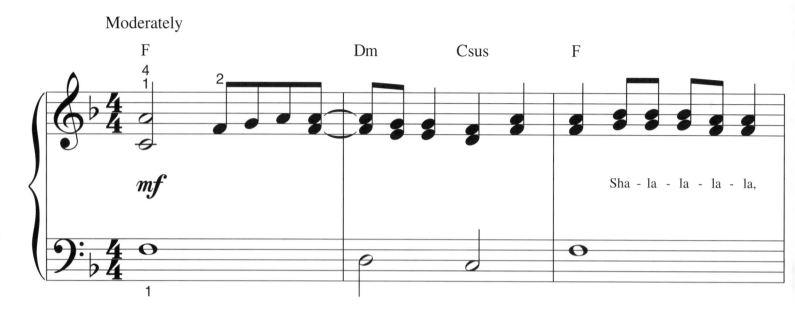

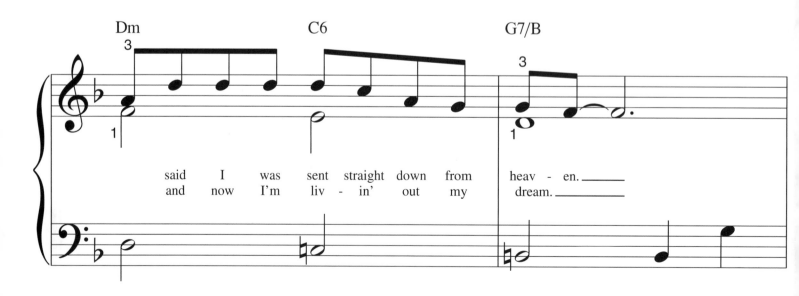